Donated by the
Franklin PTO

 W9-DBZ-181

Franklin School
Summit Public Schools

REALLY HORRIBLE FACTS

REALLY HORRIBLE HISTORY FACTS

Jay Hawkins

WINDMILL BOOKS

NEW YORK

Published in 2014 by Windmill Books, LLC
303 Park Avenue South, Suite # 1280, New York, NY 10010-3657

Copyright © 2014 by Arcturus Publishing Ltd.

All rights reserved. No part of this book may be reproduced in any form
without permission in writing from the publisher, except by a reviewer.

First Edition

Editors: Samantha Noonan, Deborah Kespert, Nicola Barber, and Joe Harris
US Editor: Joshua Shadowens
Illustrations: Dynamo Ltd, Quadrum, and Steve Beaumont
Layout design: Trudi Webb

Library of Congress Cataloging-in-Publication Data

Hawkins, Jay.
 Really horrible history facts / by Jay Hawkins.
     pages cm. -- (Really horrible facts)
 Includes index.
 ISBN 978-1-61533-746-0 (library binding) -- ISBN 978-1-61533-809-2 (pbk.) --ISBN 978-1-61533-810-8 (6-pack)
1. World history--Miscellanea--Juvenile literature. I. Title.
 D21.H394 2014
 909--dc23
                              2012049814
Printed in China
CPSIA Compliance Information: Batch #AS3102WM:
For Further Information contact Windmill Books, New York, New York at 1-866-478-0556
SL002698US

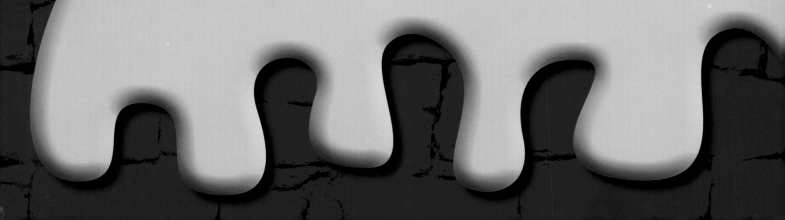

CONTENTS

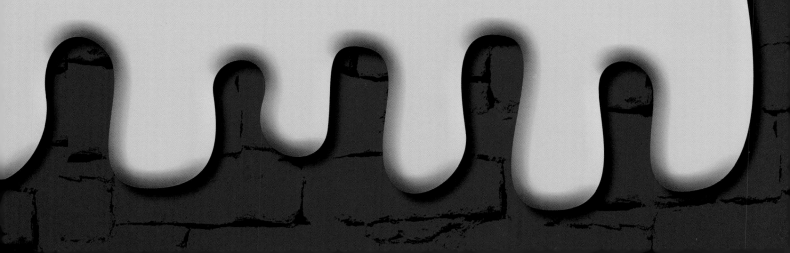

HIDEOUS HISTORY

In ancient Rome, criminals were sometimes torn apart by wild animals while the public watched. Animals were brought from all over the empire, but dogs and lions were the most popular.

In ancient Rome, urine was collected from public toilets and used as a clothes dye, a hair product, and an ingredient in toothpaste.

Ancient Romans who had killed a relative were executed by being tied in a sack with a live dog, rooster, snake, and monkey, then thrown into a river.

The Incas of South America used to mummify their dead kings and leave them sitting on their thrones.

4

Some ancient African tribes used animal dung to stiffen their hair. No point in washing it first, then!

Following Sir Walter Raleigh's execution in 1618, his wife kept Raleigh's embalmed head in a red leather bag for 29 years. She even carried it around with her until it got too smelly...

In ancient Egypt, women wore a cone of grease on their heads. During the day, the grease melted in the hot sun and dripped down, making their hair gleam.

In Jericho around 7,000 years ago, people buried their dead under the dirt floors of their houses.

Gross!

Remains found in a mass grave in South Dakota show that prehistoric warriors scalped their victims, probably to keep the hair as a trophy.

14,000 years ago, Native Americans in Florida would impale turtles on sticks and roast them over a fire.

AWESOME ANCIENT EGYPT

Pharaoh Pepy II of Egypt always kept several slaves with him whose bodies were smeared with honey. This encouraged flies to land on them instead of on him. No flies on that pharaoh!

Gross!

Before embalming the body, a pharaoh's vital organs (the lungs, liver, stomach, and intestines) were removed and stored in special jars in the tomb.

Careless embalmers accidentally wrapped flies, lizards, and even a mouse into some mummies' bandages!

GRUESOME GREEKS

The ancient Greeks didn't use napkins. Instead they wiped their hands on pieces of bread, then fed the bread to the dogs.

A sumptuous feast in ancient Greece might include any of these yummy morsels: sea urchins, thrushes, peacock eggs, grasshoppers, or pigs that had died from eating too much.

Both the ancient Greeks and Romans believed they could tell the future by examining the patterns made by the guts spilled from sacrificed birds. The future always looked grim for the birds...

Many ancient Greek Olympic events were carried out naked. Hmm...!

Greek physicians were first permitted to dissect bodies around 2,000 years ago. They were also allowed to perform vivisection (the cutting up of live bodies) on criminals.

An ancient Greek cure for bad breath was to boil the head of a hare together with three mice then rub the resulting mixture on the gums. It probably covered up the original smell, but wasn't necessarily any better!

REVOLTING ROMANS

Roman whips were especially vicious—they had pieces of bone or metal on their ends.

To clean themselves, Romans poured olive oil all over their bodies then scraped off the oily, dirty gunk with a curved blade called a strigil. Yuck!

People living in the ancient Italian town of Pompeii were trapped under piles of volcanic ash after Mount Vesuvius erupted in AD 79. When the bodies decomposed, they left their shapes behind in the hardened ash. Two thousand years later, plaster casts were made of the shapes.

Galen, an ancient Roman physician, was a pioneer of cataract surgery. He used long needles on sufferers' eyes. This was in the days before anesthesia!

Under the Roman king Tarquinius Priscus, people who committed suicide were crucified... even though they were already dead!

Ancient Romans spread pigeon droppings on their hair to lighten it—the ammonia acted as a bleach. You wouldn't have wanted to work in a hairdresser's in those days...

Roman gladiators had to fight to the bitter end—any who stopped would be prodded with hot pokers to spur them on again.

13

MONSTROUS MIDDLE AGES

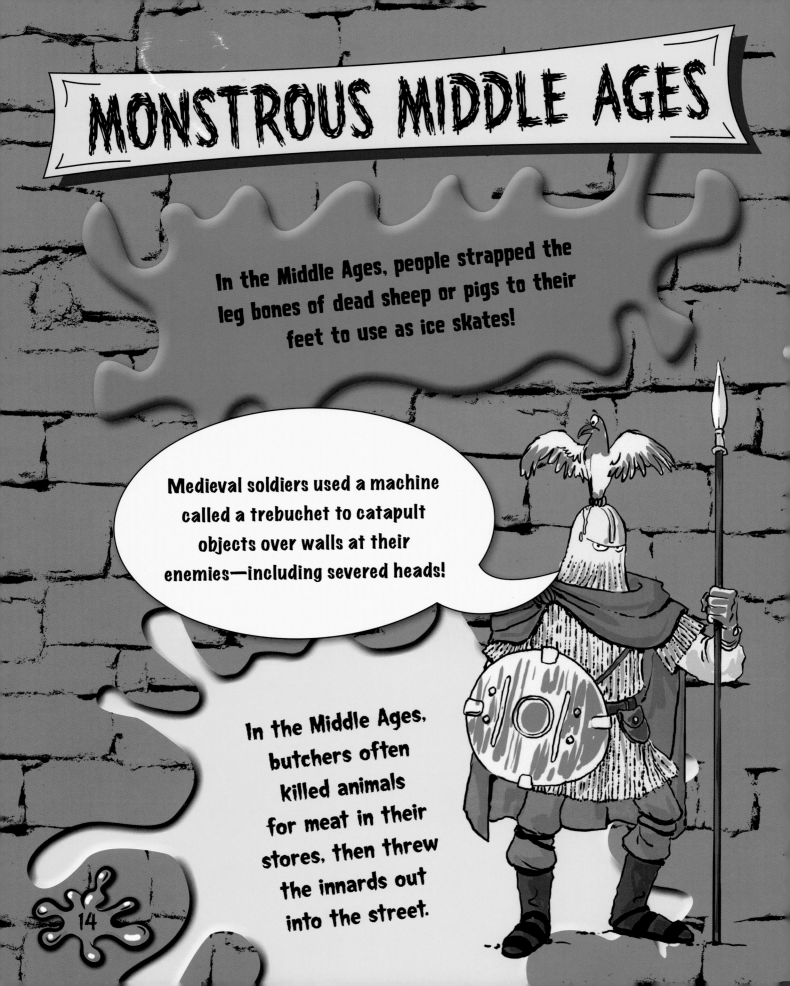

In the Middle Ages, people strapped the leg bones of dead sheep or pigs to their feet to use as ice skates!

Medieval soldiers used a machine called a trebuchet to catapult objects over walls at their enemies—including severed heads!

In the Middle Ages, butchers often killed animals for meat in their stores, then threw the innards out into the street.

Some medieval kings employed a royal farter. The job of the farter was to amuse the king by jumping around and farting.

In the Middle Ages, people made washing powder from wood ash and urine.

In Anglo-Saxon England, people who died in a famine were sometimes eaten by their neighbors!

The plague of Justinian spread all over Europe between AD 541 and 542. At its worst it killed between 5,000 and 10,000 people every day. Often, there wasn't enough room to bury the dead, so bodies were left rotting in the streets.

MAD MODERN TIMES

During World War II, the Soviet army used dogs strapped with explosives to blow up German tanks.

After the death of Vladimir Lenin in 1924, his brain was entrusted to a respected doctor who (it was hoped) would one day be able to revive the Soviet leader...

During the civil war in Liberia, Africa, of 1989-1996, General Joshua Milton Blahyi was famous for leading his army into battle naked—except for his boots and gun. His nickname was "General Butt-Naked"!

Toilet paper first appeared in the shops in 1928.

The first animal in space was a dog called Laika, sent into orbit in the Soviet satellite Sputnik 2 in 1957. Laika didn't survive the journey, but will be remembered in the history books forever!

The world's biggest food fight started in 1944. It still happens every year on the last Wednesday of August. The town of Buñol, Spain, hosts an annual festival called La Tomatina in which 40,000 people pelt each other with tomatoes!

17

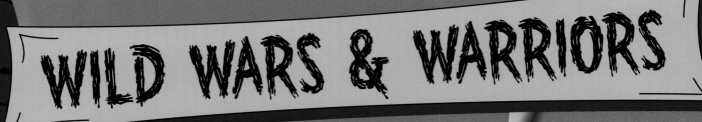

Gross!

New Scythian soldiers had to drink the blood of the first enemy soldier they killed.

When the British warrior-queen Boudicca marched on the Roman town of Londinium (London), her army killed 70,000 people.

Medieval suits of armor could be a danger in themselves. Some knights baked to death when they were fighting in hot countries!

18

When the first emperor of China died in 210 BC, an army of 7,500 terracotta soldiers was placed in his tomb at Xianyang. It was also booby-trapped, so that anyone who tried to break through the hillside doorway would be shot with an arrow.

If they were feeling really bloodthirsty, Vikings would kill enemies using the "blood eagle"— the victim's ribs would be cut and opened out, then the lungs would be removed. How horrible!

Yuck!

The terrifying 15th-century warrior Pier Gerlofs Donia was known for his ability to chop off several enemies' heads with one swing of his great sword.

DEATH AND DISEASE

One symptom of smallpox was black pox—the skin took on a charred appearance, turning black and peeling off.

In the 1800s, there were several cases of people being buried alive. Terrible stories about opened coffins with scratch marks on the inside, or corpses with fingernails worn away by trying to escape, led to cautious people being buried with a system of warning bells fitted in the coffin, which they could ring if they woke up.

In the 17th and 18th centuries, plague doctors wore special masks with long beaks. The beaks were filled with herbs, flowers, and straw.

In the 19th century, London had a train service for the dead! Mourners and coffin bearers would depart from Necropolis Station and get off at Cemetery Station, near where funerals were held in Brookwood Cemetery.

A terrible plague killed a third of the population of Athens in 430 BC. Victims had a fever, headaches, stomach pain, vomiting, diarrhea, and were covered in painful blisters. Those that didn't die often lost fingers, toes, or their sight. Historians still don't know what the disease was.

TERRIBLE TREATMENTS

Ancient Egyptian physicians used acacia thorns as needles when they stitched up wounds.

A popular Victorian beauty treatment contained arsenic, vinegar, and chalk. What's a little arsenic poisoning if you have perfect skin?

An early typhus vaccine was made from squashed body lice infected with the deadly disease!

People have always had tooth decay! In ancient times, they believed that a "tooth worm" ate the teeth and left holes behind.

22

Eighteenth-century toothpaste recipes included burnt bread and dragon's blood. It's not quite as gruesome as it sounds—dragon's blood was a red plant resin.

Some surgeons in ancient times tried using pig skin for nose reconstructions on people. When the skin shriveled up and dropped off, they believed it was because the pig had died!

Blood-sucking leeches were first used as a medical treatment by the ancient Egyptians. In the Middle Ages, they were used to treat many different ailments, including headaches!

SLAUGHTER & TORTURE

Gross!

A Chinese torture chair from the 19th century has blades sticking up from the armrests and seat, and sticking out from the back. It would be impossible to sit on it without being stabbed—your own weight would push the blades into your flesh.

Samurai swords were rated for sharpness by how many (dead) human bodies they could slice through in one go. The best swords scored a rating of five bodies.

The Celts, who lived in Britain around 500 BC, collected the heads of people they slaughtered in battle. They stuck them on poles, chucked them in rivers as gifts to the gods, nailed them to the walls as decorations, or hollowed them out to use as cups. You'd think their drinks would run out through the eyeholes...

24

When Genghis Khan laid siege to the city of Volohai, he demanded 1,000 cats and 10,000 swallows from the inhabitants. He then tied flaming cloths to their tails and set the animals free, setting fire to the city as they went.

A French medieval torture involved trapping a person in the stocks, pouring salt water over their bare feet, and letting a goat lick it off. The goat's rough tongue would soon start to strip the flesh from the victim's feet.

During the siege of Megara, Greece, the Megarians poured oil over a herd of pigs, set fire to them, then drove the pigs toward the war elephants of their enemies. The elephants bolted in terror from the squealing pigs and trampled the enemy soldiers.

CRIME AND PUNISHMENT

In 1750 BC, the Babylonian king Hammurabi established a particularly harsh set of laws. Punishments included cutting off a finger or hand for theft and cutting off a man's lower lip for kissing a married woman.

Public hangings were stopped in England in 1868. They had become so crowded that too many people were being hurt or killed in the crush to see the action!

Chicago gangster Dion O'Banion was given a lavish funeral in 1924, with 10,000 mourners paying their respects. The biggest and most expensive wreath came from Al Capone—the gangster who had ordered O'Banion's murder!

26

The 17th-century Italian lady's poison of choice was Acqua Toffana: a lethal cocktail of arsenic, lead, and belladonna (deadly nightshade). Perfect for using on an annoying husband!

A medieval punishment for murderers was to have each arm and leg tied to a different horse. Then the four horses were made to run in different directions, tearing the criminal apart.

In 1924, the state of Nevada introduced the gas chamber as a more humane form of execution. Its first victim was convicted murderer Gee Jong.

The most common punishments in the Middle Ages were death, exile, and mutilation—lovely!

Mongol leader Tamerlane played polo with the skulls of people he had killed in battle.

When Ivan the Terrible found out his sixth wife was having an affair, he had her boyfriend impaled on a spike and left to die outside her bedroom window.

It is said that Attila the Hun (who ruled the Hun kingdom in AD 434–453) enjoyed the taste of raw flesh and human blood. Saves on cooking...

On October 25, 1760, King George II became the second English king to die on the toilet.

28

The most notorious pirate was Edward Teach (1680—1718), known as Blackbeard. He would leap into action with exploding firecrackers tied to his bushy black beard.

Naturalist William Buckland liked exotic food. Among his favorite meals were elephant's trunk soup, roast giraffe, and panther chops. He even tried earwigs once, but complained they tasted rather bitter.

English highway robber Dick Turpin's career ended when he was arrested for shooting his landlord's rooster. He was hanged in York in 1739.

REPULSIVE ROYALTY

King Francis I of France, who ruled between 1515 and 1547, always carried with him a small piece of an ancient Egyptian mummy! He used it as a medicine to soothe bruises.

Gross!

Tudor King Henry VIII reigned over England from 1509 until his death in 1547. He married six times. The lucky ones escaped with divorce—two had their heads chopped off!

After William the Conqueror's death in 1087, his body swelled up with gas as he started to decompose. On the day of his funeral, his stomach exploded, causing a terrible stench. Unable to close the coffin lid, the bishops conducted one of the fastest royal funerals ever recorded.

30

Queen Elizabeth I had very bad teeth, but was so afraid of having one taken out that a loyal Archbishop had to have one of his teeth removed first to reassure her.

Henry VIII's second wife, Anne Boleyn, was born with eleven fingers.

Hung Wu, the first emperor of the Ming dynasty in China, was so fearful of the rebellious city of Peiping, that in 1368 he ordered the entire city to be destroyed.

Yuck!

Fierce Catholic Mary I of England, known as "Bloody Mary," executed more than 200 Protestants when she reigned over England between 1553 and 1558.

GLOSSARY

anesthesia *(a-nus-THEE-zhuh)*
Using drugs to stop you feeling pain.

arsenic *(AR-sih-nik)* *A poisonous chemical.*

cataract *(KA-teh-rakt)* *A cloudy patch in the lens of the eye that blurs vision and can lead to blindness.*

embalm *(em-BAHLM)* *To preserve a dead body in order to stop it rotting.*

impale *(im-PAHL)* *To pierce something with a sharp point.*

vaccine *(vak-SEEN)* *This gives someone a mild form of an illness to protect them from a more serious form.*

FURTHER READING

Allen, Kathy. *The Horrible, Miserable Middle Ages.* Mankato, MN: Capstone Press, 2011.

Armstrong, Jennifer. *The American Story.* New York: Knopf Books, 2006.

Pipe, Jim. *You Wouldn't Want to be Cleopatra!* New York: Children's Press, 2007.

WEBSITES

For web resources related to the subject of this book, go to: www.windmillbooks.com/weblinks and select this book's title.

INDEX